LET'S INVESTIGATE

Codes
and Sequences

LET'S INVESTIGATE
Codes
and
Sequences

By Marion Smoothey
Illustrated by Ann Baum

MARSHALL CAVENDISH
NEW YORK · LONDON · TORONTO · SYDNEY

© Marshall Cavendish Corporation 1995

Published by Marshall Cavendish Corporation
2415 Jerusalem Avenue
PO Box 587
North Bellmore
New York 11710

Series created by Graham Beehag Books

Editorial consultant: Prof. Sonia Helton
University of South Florida, St. Petersburg

Library of Congress Cataloging-in-Publication Data

Smoothey, Marion,
     Codes and sequences / by Marion Smoothey :
     illustrated by Ann Baum. – Library ed.
        p. cm. – (Lets Investigate)
     Includes index.
     ISBN 1-85435-774-3 ISBN 1-854535-773-5 (set)
     1. Cryptography – Juvenile literature. [1. Cryptography.]
     I. Baum, Ann. ill. II. Title. III. Series: Smoothey, Marion, 1943-
     Lets Investigate.
     Z103.3.S66 1995   94-13134
     6522'.8 – dc20   CIP
                                                AC

Printed in Malaysia by Times Offset (M) SDN BHD

Contents

Introduction

While you are reading any book you are cracking a code without realizing it. The letters in it are just marks on paper. You have learned that they stand for sounds and make words.

During World War II, the Navajo Indians were considered to be some of the greatest code talkers. The Japanese were unable to decode the Navajo language. This book introduces you to a few of the less familiar codes that people, across the world, and through the centuries, have invented. It shows you how to be a code cracker and how to invent your own codes. When you have read it and decoded its messages, you will have learned how we often use codes in daily life.

Lisa is sending a message to her friend Becky.

● What does she have in common with Julius Caesar?

When you are figuring the answers, write the coded message on a separate sheet of paper so you can work on it. Do not write on the book.

Mirror Writing

8

Like Julius Caesar, Lisa has sent a message in a different form from ordinary language. Lisa has done this because she wants only Becky to be able to read the message. She has used a cipher, or code.

Her cipher is very simple. She has written the letters back to front, as they would appear in a mirror, and has not left any spaces between the words or used punctuation marks.

- **1.** What does Lisa's message say?
- **2.** Why did she leave out the punctuation and the spaces between the words?

Nulls

A **null** is a letter that is not part of the message. It can be put in to show the breaks between words. More often, nulls are used to confuse anyone who is trying to break a secret cipher.

- **3.** Write out Lisa's message grouping the letters in fours and using F as a null between each word.

Substitution Ciphers

Julius Caesar's Cipher

Julius Caesar, the great Roman general and emperor, fought many wars in Gaul. Gaul was roughly the same region as today's France. When he needed to send reports back to Rome, he used a secret cipher. He did this so the contents of the reports would remain secret even if his messengers were intercepted by the enemy.

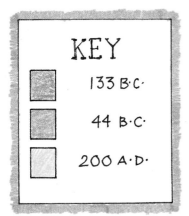

His cipher was a very simple one. The Roman alphabet had 22 letters.

A B C D E F G H I L M N O P Q R S T U V X Z

● What are the missing letters?
Julius Caesar rewrote the alphabet moving each letter along three positions, like this:

A B C D E F G H I L M N O P Q R S T U V X Z
D E F G H I L M N O P Q R S T U V X Z A B C

This is called **a substitution** cipher because it works by substituting one letter for another.

Caesar wrote in Latin. If he wanted to send the message, *``Nostri victoria potiti sunt.''* (``Our soldiers gained the victory.''), he would write:

QRVXUN ANFXRUND SRXNXN VZQX

10

If Caesar left out the spaces between the words, it would be even more difficult for an enemy who captured the messenger to decode the message.

In this case, Nostri victoria potiti sunt becomes

QRVXUNANFXRUNDSRXNXNVZQX

● **1.** Rewrite this, grouping the letters in fives and using S as a null to mark the end of each word.

● **2.** How can you group the message, using nulls, so that each group is the same length?

Try decoding these messages from Caesar's code. They are written in English!

● **3.** QHHGUHNQIRFHPHQXV

● **4.** NVMDOOINLMXDXGDXINUVXONLMX

● **5.** MDAHOF DSXZUH GOXMHO LDZOVO OHDGHU

Making a Cipher Wheel

The trouble with using this kind of cipher is that it is very easy to break. You can make a device that will crack any substitution cipher. It is also useful for sending ciphered messages.

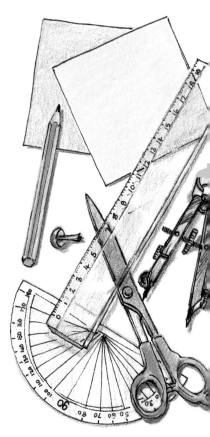

This device was first invented by an Italian architect, Leon Battista Alberti, in the 15th century. Americans used brass versions of it in the Civil War.

You need a compass, a protractor, a pencil, a ruler, scissors, a paper fastener, and two pieces of cardboard.

On separate pieces of cardboard, draw two circles, one with a **radius** of 2 inches and one with a radius of 2 inches.

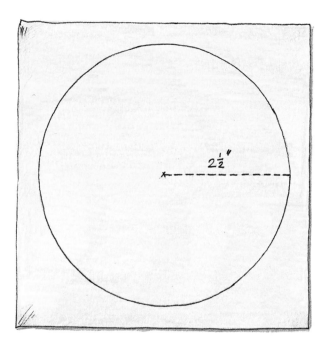

$2\frac{1}{2}''$

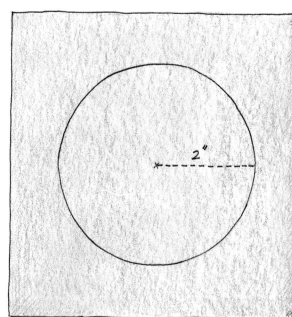

$2''$

Divide each circle into 26 equal sectors, one for each letter of the alphabet. A circle has 360 degrees: 26 will not divide exactly into 360, but if you check with a calculator you will see that 360 ÷ 26 is very nearly equal to 14 degrees.

Use your protractor to mark off 13 **sectors** of 14 degrees on your large circle.

13

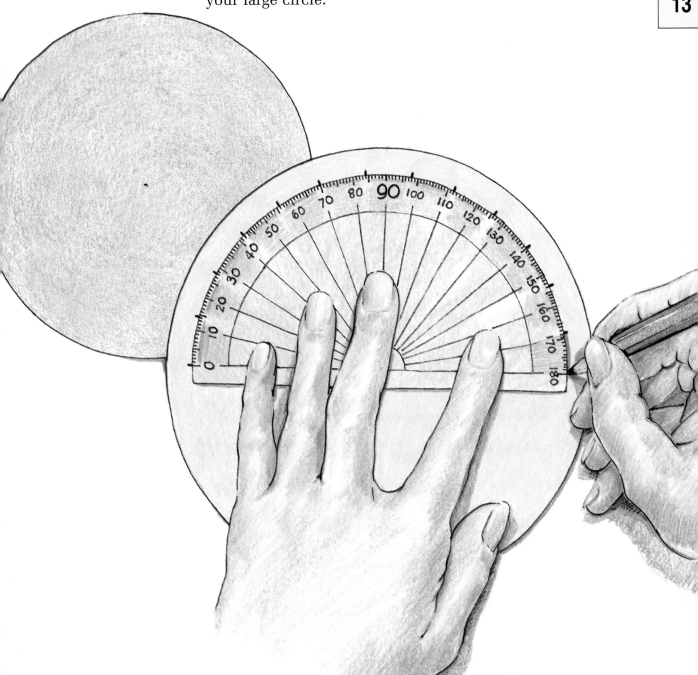

Using your 13 marks, you can then carefully draw lines with a ruler from each side of the **circumference** through the center of the large circle to make 26 sectors.

14

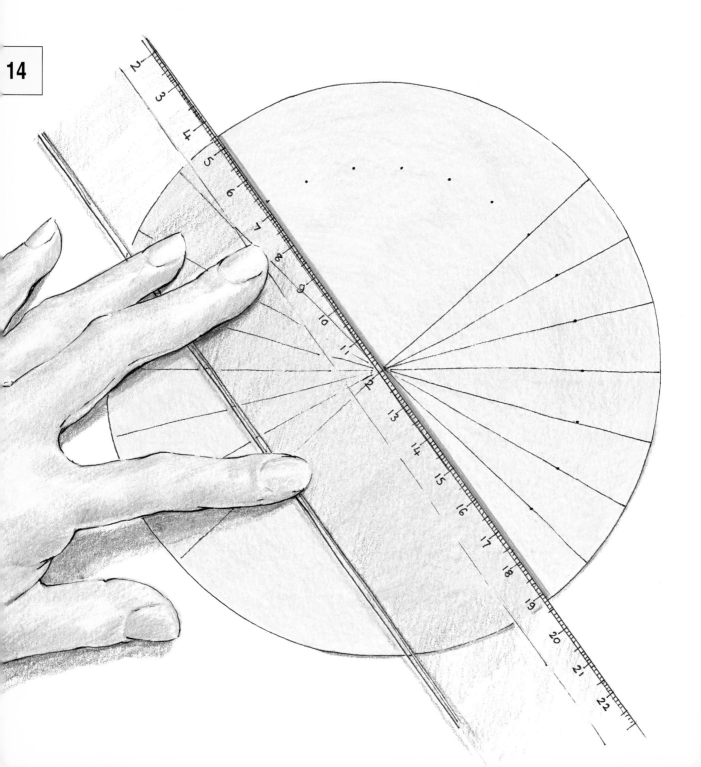

1. Pierce the centers of each circle with your compass point.

2. Lay the smaller circle on top of the larger one, with the centers matching.

3. Insert the paper fastener and attach the two circles together so that the top one rotates freely.

4. Use the lines on the larger circle to mark off 26 matching sectors on the smaller circle.

5. Fill in the letters of the alphabet, in the correct order, in the spaces on the circumferences of each of the circles.

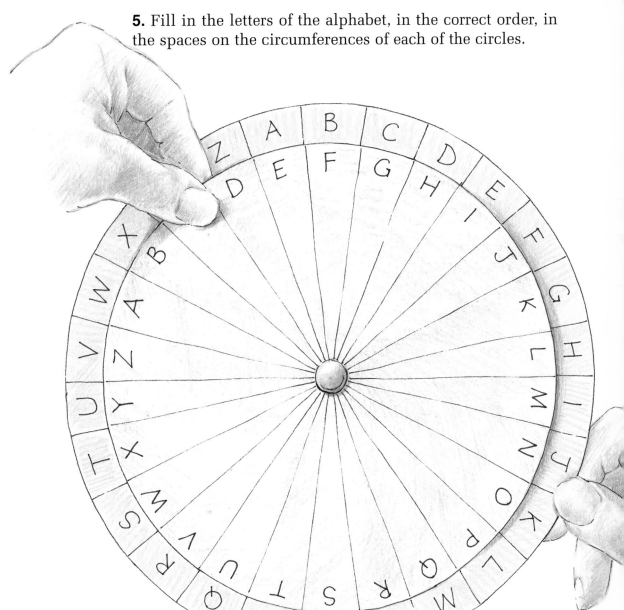

Using a Cipher Wheel

To send or receive messages, simply turn the inner circle so that whatever letter you choose to stand for **A** is aligned with **A** on the outer circle. Begin with the letters on the two circles matching each other – **A** to **A**, **B** to **B**, and so on. Decide how many places you want to move the letters, and turn the inner circle. If you decide to move the letters five places, **A** will become **V** if you turn the inner circle clockwise.

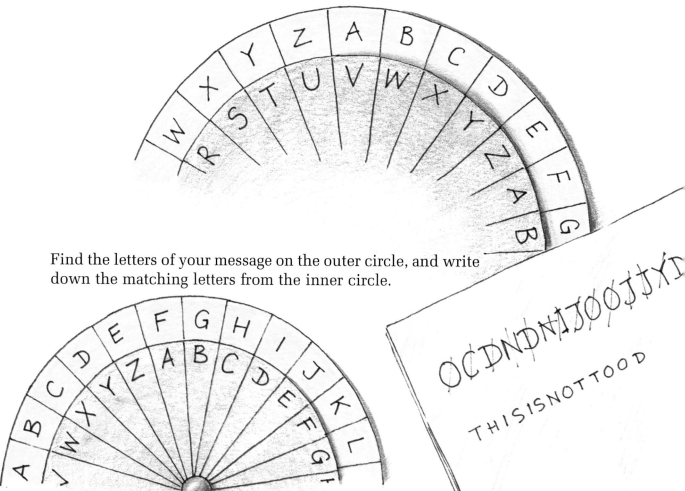

Find the letters of your message on the outer circle, and write down the matching letters from the inner circle.

● **1.** What will **A** become if you turn the inner circle five places counter-clockwise?

● **2.** How many spaces do you have to turn the inner wheel clockwiseto get the same cipher?

● **3.** How many ciphers can you make using this wheel?

It is much easier to decipher a message if you know how many places the letters have been moved and whether to work clockwise or counter-clockwise. (Every cipher can be made by turning the circle clockwise, but it is easier to turn the shortest way.)

You can work it out by trial and error, but it might take a long time!

An easy way to convey this information is to tell the receiver of the message which letter is equivalent to A. This can be done by inserting it as a null in an agreed position in the coded message.

If you received this message:

18

MEET ME AT 5 O'CLOCK UZRD RFEU JRIV TVZM VURJ RWVC PR

you would guess that 5 was a clue and that the real message was in the ciphered part.

The fifth letter in the ciphered message is R, so the wheel is set like this:

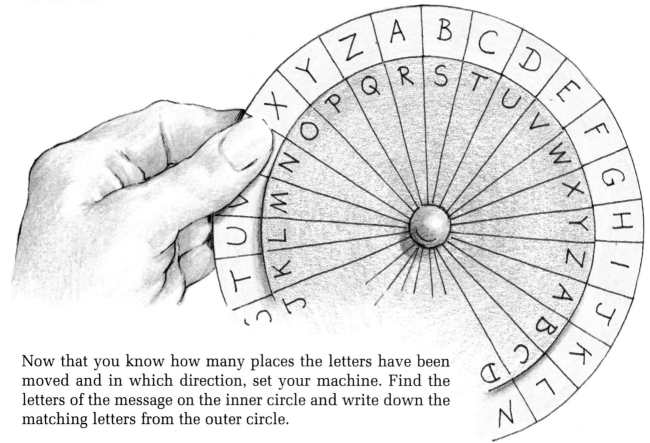

Now that you know how many places the letters have been moved and in which direction, set your machine. Find the letters of the message on the inner circle and write down the matching letters from the outer circle.

● What does the message say?

● What do these messages say?

1. RTAJJFHMQJYYJWKNAJUQFHJX (Five places, counter-clockwise)

2. MXUHUMEKBTOEKJQAUQIYSAXEHIU (Ten places, clockwise)

3. SNZGNROHSZK (One place, clockwise)

Try sending some messages of your own.

19

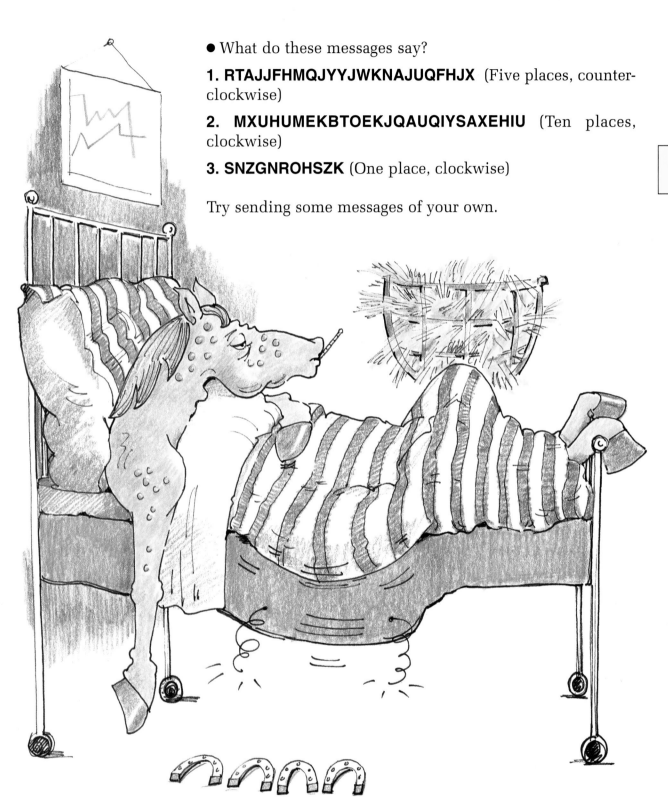

Investigating Cipher Wheels

You can make a different kind of cipher wheel by writing the alphabet counter-clockwise on the inner wheel.

● **1.** How many different ciphers are possible with the top wheel?

The lower wheel has been set for one of the possible ciphers.

● **2.** Look at **A** on the outer wheel and find its matching cipher letter on the inner wheel. Now look at **S** on the outer wheel. What do you notice?

● **3.** Try the same thing for **E** and **O**. Does the same thing happen?

Try it for other pairs of letters.

● **4.** What do you notice about the code letter for **W**?

● **5.** Does this happen anywhere else?

● **6.** How many letters are there between each matching pair?

There are 26 possible ciphers using the cipher wheel when the inner wheel has the alphabet written counter-clockwise on it.

● **1.** Why is there one extra cipher on the counter-clockwise wheel?

Look at the way the wheel has been set this time.

● **2.** When the wheel is set like this, how many pairs of letters are the same on the inner and outer wheels?

● **3.** Look at the code letter for F. What is the code letter for W? What do you notice?

● **4.** Does the same thing happen for all the other letters?

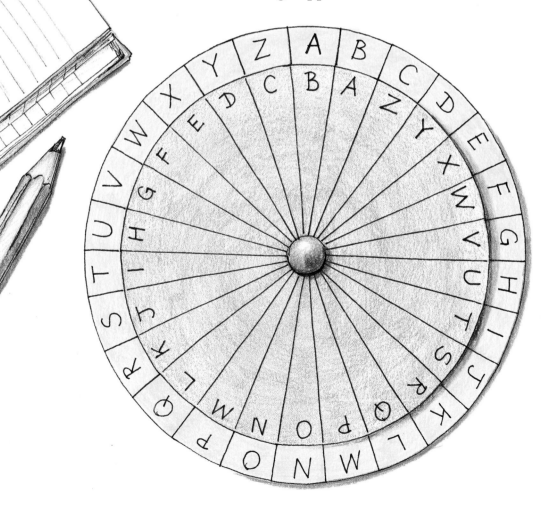

You will find it easier to answer these questions if you take apart your code wheel. Write the alphabet counter-clockwise on the back of the inner wheel, and then put it back together.

● **1.** Which letters match on both wheels when the code letter for **A** is **C**?

● **2.** Which code letters match on both wheels when the code letter for **A** is **D**?

● **3.** Predict which letters match when the code letter for **A** is **E**.

● **4.** If you move the inner wheel an odd number of spaces from **A**, do you get matching pairs of letters?

● **5.** How many positions are there that give matching pairs of letters?

22

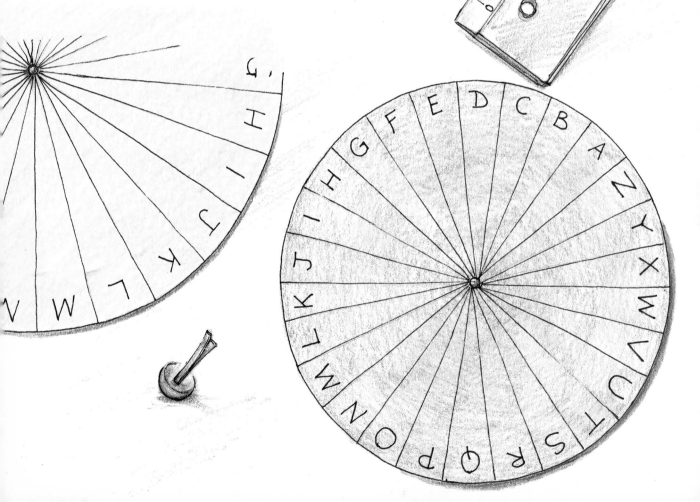

Random Ciphers

Substitution cipherscan be made harder to break by mixing up the letters in a random way. For example:

A B C D E F G H I J K L M N O P Q R S T U V W X Y Z

E H S A N K B C L O Q D F W R G I M P T V Z J U Y X

The trouble with this is that anyone receiving the coded message would need a copy of the equivalent letters; it is hard to memorize all 26 letters when there is no pattern. If you were using Alberti's disk, you would need one with the jumbled letters on the inner circle.

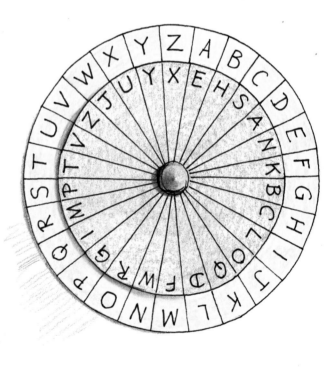

● **1.** How many different codes can be made using this disk?
● **2.** How can you show which of the codes to use?

This could be dangerous if secrecy was important. Once the decoder was found and copied by the enemy, any message could be quickly read. This is a danger when any type of code is written down.

In the Second World War, the British recovered German code books from sunken submarines. With the help of the books, the British were able to intercept and decode secret messages about German naval operations.

Code Words

One way to avoid the problem of remembering a random cipher is to have a code word for the first letters of the alphabet, and then to use the rest of the alphabet in order.

If the code word is FOREIGN, the code works like this:

First write out the alphabet.

A B C D E F G H I J K L M N O P Q R S T U V WX Y Z

Write out the code word underneath the first letters.

A B C D E F G.....

F O R E I G N....

Continue the second line by using, in alphabetical order, all the letters not already used in the code word.

A B C D E F G H I J K L M N O P Q R S T U V W X Y Z

F O R E I G N A B C D H J K L M P Q S T U V W X Y Z

You can use words that repeat letters. You just omit the repeated letters when setting out the code. If we change the code words to FOREIGN AGENT, we use the letters FOREIGNAT.

The code now becomes:

A B C D E F G H I J K L M N O P Q R S T U V W X Y Z

F O R E I G N A T B C D H J K L M P Q S U V W X Y Z

You will notice that in each case, the letters at the end of the alphabet stay the same.

The person receiving the coded message has to memorize only the code word to be able to work out the rest of the code. He does not need to keep a copy of it, which could fall into enemy hands.

The code word is HUMOROUS.

- **1. WBHQURQMHIQRVRNURWJI**
- **2. QBRHFKBHURQ**

Why couldn't the SKELETON go to the ball?

- **3. ATASLHIKILYRINIWBRA**

26

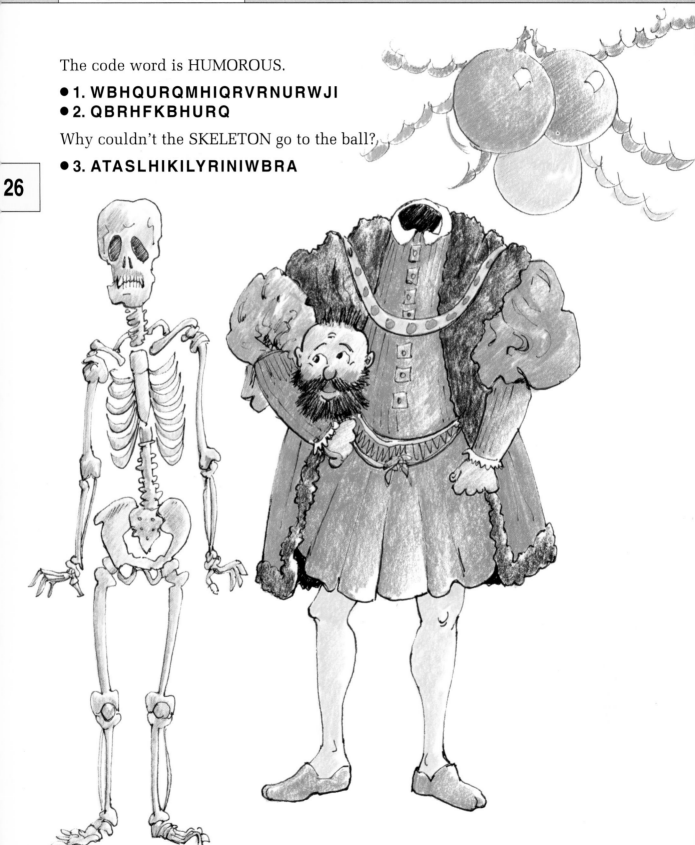

Codes Using Numbers for Letters

27

You can also make codes using numbers to stand for the letters of the alphabet. These codes can be very simple or quite complex. A simple version is to just use the counting numbers.

A B C D E F G H I J K L M N O P Q R S T ...

1 2 3 4 5 6 7 8 9 10 11 12 13 14 15 16 17 18 19 20 ....

● Can you answer this?

**9 6 9 20 20 1 11 5 19 20 5 14 13 5 14 6 15 21 18
4 1 25 19 20 15 4 9 7 1 8 15 12 5 8 15 23 12 15 14
7 23 9 12 12 9 20 20 1 11 5 6 9 22 5 13 5 14 20 15
4 9 7 8 1 12 6 1 8 15 12 5**

This code is easy to break, especially when spaces are left between each number. You can make a harder code by carrying out arithmetical operations on the counting numbers. For example, you can multiply each of the counting numbers by 3. This is the same as using the three times table. **A** is 3, **B** is 6, **C** is 9, and so on.

● **1.** What will **Z** be? Do not write out the whole alphabet.

28

If you use a combination of multiplication and addition or subtraction on the counting numbers, then the code becomes very difficult to guess. For example, if you multiply each counting number by 3 and then subtract 2, you get

A B C D E F G H I J K L M...

1   4   7 10 13 16 ...

● **2.** Finish writing out the code and use it to decode this message.

**67 22 1 58 55 67 43 52 55 13 58 22 1 40 16 25 40 10 25 40 19 1 67
43 52 37 43 58 25 40 1 40 1 46 46 34 13**

● **3.** 16 25 40 10 25 40 19 22 1 34 16 1 67 43 52 37

● **4.** Why is it not a good idea to use division?

What has been done to the counting numbers in these sequences?

● **1.** 2 7 12 17 22

● **2.** 0 4 8 12 16

● **3.** 8 10 12 14 16

● **4.** Can you answer this? You can work out which of the codes above has been used if you look carefully at the numbers in the message. The illustration should help you.

88 28 0 76 12 56 96 56 80 24 16 76 32 20 96 56 80 8 68 56 72 72 0 72 52 56 88 4 0 44 44 88 32 76 28 0 72 28 0 68 40

It is still pretty easy to break this kind of code because the numbers go up in regular jumps. In the code used for the joke on page 23, the numbers go up in 3's.

● How much do the numbers in questions 1 to 3 on page 29 go up by?

Turn back to question 2 on page 28. If you write out in ascending order one of each of the numbers that have been used you get:

1 10 13 16 19 22 25 34 37 40 43 46 52 55 58 67

It is fairly obvious that the numbers go up in threes, if you look at the groups 10 13 16 19 22 25, then 34 37 40 43 46 and 52 55 58.

It is also likely that **1** stands for **A**. It is now simple to write out the whole code and decode the message.

● **1.   Question:** 36 24 4 16 60 28 36 76 80 36 20 16
80 60 4 72 60 64 20 24 36 24 80 20 20 56 24 20 20
80 48 60 56 28, 32 60 92 12 4 56 36 80 72 20 4 12
32 4 8 60 56 20 80 32 36 72 80 100 24 20 20 80 4
92 4 100?

● **2.** What is the size of the jump between the letters?

● **3.** What number stands for **A**

● **4.**   Answer: **80 32 20 72 60 64 20 36 76 56 80 60
80 36 20 16 80 60 4 56 100 80 32 36 56 28**

Using Grids

One way to make a number code that is harder to break is to arrange the letters of the alphabet in a 5 by 5 grid and use a pair of numbers for each letter. The advantage is that you do not have to leave spaces between the numbers, because all the letters are two numbers.

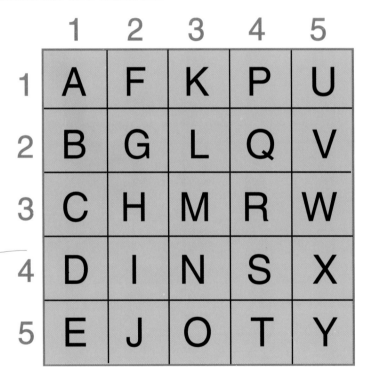

	1	2	3	4	5
1	A	F	K	P	U
2	B	G	L	Q	V
3	C	H	M	R	W
4	D	I	N	S	X
5	E	J	O	T	Y

● **1.** What is the disadvantage of this method? How many letters can you fit into a 5 by 5 grid?

A becomes **11, B** is **21, C** is **31, M** is **33, U** is **15**, and so on.

● **2.** How do you write ENEMY SIGHTED using this code?

A Scytale

There is another device for sending and receiving messages in code. All you need is two matching cardboard tubes from rolls of paper towels or aluminum foil and some paper cut into strips about 1 inch wide and joined together.

The sender wraps the paper around one of the tubes and writes the message.

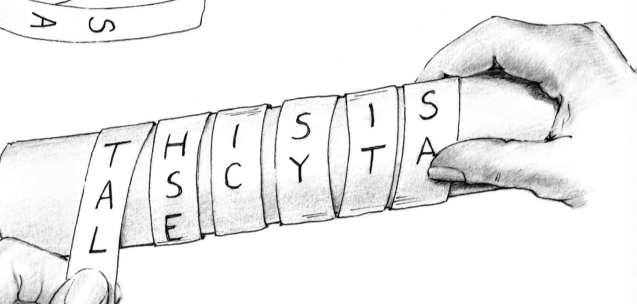

The sender then unwraps the strip and sends it to the receiver. The receiver wraps the strip around his tube to decode the message.

It is believed that the ancient Greeks and Romans used scytales.

● How can you figure out the size of tube you need to decode a scytale message?

Letter Frequency

Investigation

Making a frequency table

On a piece of lined paper, draw three columns, the first narrow, the second wide, and the last narrow. Head the columns Letter, Tally, and Frequency. In the first column, write down the letters of the alphabet in order, one letter to a line.

Turn to page 16 and look at the first sentence beginning ``To send or receive messages..''. Make a tally mark in the second column on the matching line of your paper each time a letter appears in the sentence.

After the first four words, your **frequency** table should look like the one illustrated.

Remember to put a horizontal stroke through four vertical strokes to show five: this makes it easier to tally up the frequencies at the end.

When you have completed your tally of the letters of the words in the sentence, total the tally marks for each letter and enter the results in the Frequency column.

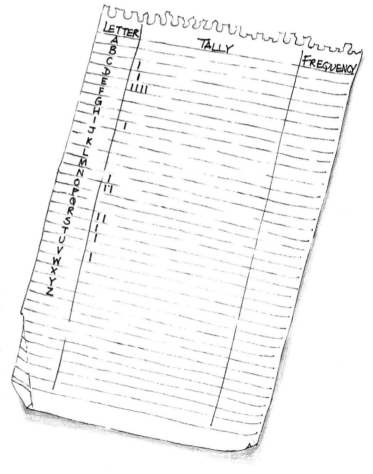

Making a Bar Chart

Turn to page 36 to check your frequency table.

To make the information in your frequency table easier to interpret, you can use it to make a bar chart. Turn a piece of graph paper sideways and mark off 26 equal spaces for the letters of the alphabet along the bottom. Label each space with its letter.

☙ What is the largest number in the frequency column of your table?

Make a numbered scale up the left hand side of the paper. Make sure that your scale goes up far enough for the largest number on your frequency table.
Label this scale FREQUENCY.

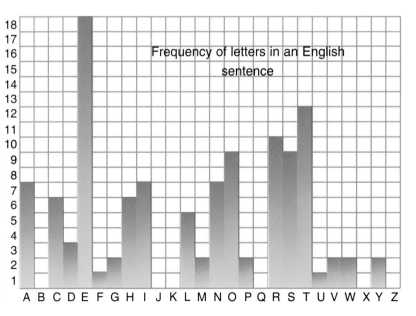

Frequency of letters in an English sentence

Use your frequency table to draw the columns for the bar chart. The bar for **A** will reach as far as 7 on your scale, but **B** will not have a bar at all because it has a frequency of zero.

When you have drawn your bars, color them in and give your bar chart a title.

Your frequency table for the letters in the sentence from page 16 should look like this.

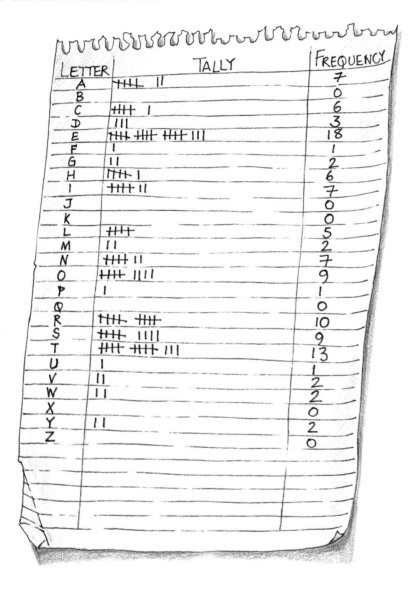

LETTER	TALLY	FREQUENCY
A	ＨＨＬ ＩＩ	7
B		0
C	ＨＨＴ Ｉ	6
D	ＩＩＩ	3
E	ＴＨＴ ＨＨＴ ＨＨＴ ＩＩＩ	18
F	Ｉ	1
G	ＩＩ	2
H	ＨＨＬ Ｉ	6
I	ＴＨＨＴ ＩＩ	7
J		0
K		0
L	ＨＨＴ	5
M	ＩＩ	2
N	ＨＨＴ ＩＩ	7
O	ＨＨＴ ＩＩＩＩ	9
P	Ｉ	1
Q		0
R	ＴＨＨＬ ＨＨＴ	10
S	ＨＨＴ ＩＩＩＩ	9
T	ＨＨＴ ＨＨＴ ＩＩＩ	13
U	Ｉ	1
V	ＩＩ	2
W	ＩＩ	2
X		0
Y	ＩＩ	2
Z		0

Average Frequency of Letters

This bar chart shows the approximate percentage frequency for each letter in English. Each percentage has been rounded up or down to the nearest whole number.

● If you add up the percentages for each letter what should the total be?

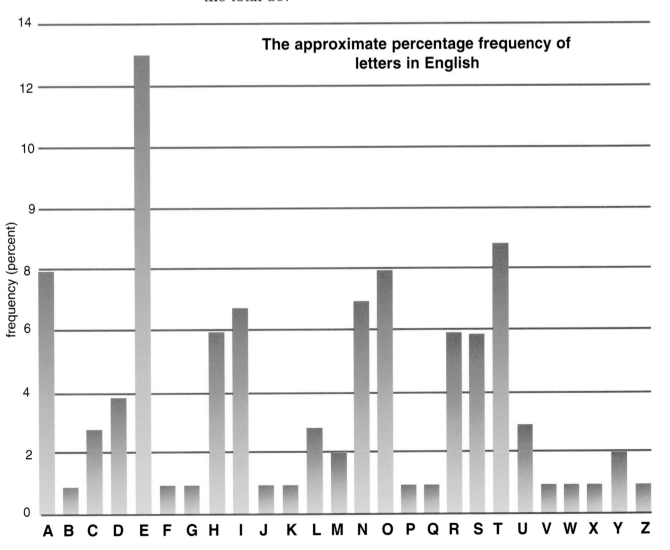

The approximate percentage frequency of letters in English

● **1.** Write out the first four letters in order of frequency in the chart on the opposite page.

● **2.** What are the 11 least frequently used letters in English according to the chart?

Compare this bar chart with the one you have just made.

● **3.** Are the four most frequent letters the same in both charts?

● **4.** Are the 13 least frequent letters the same in both charts?

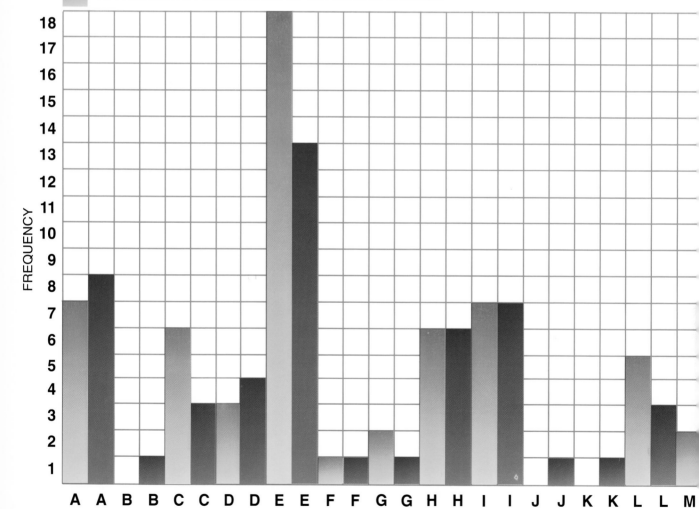

FREQUENCY OF LETTERS IN AN ENGLISH SENTENCE

APPROXIMATE PRECENTAGE OF LETTERS IN ENGLISH

On these two pages you can see the two bar charts together. Remember that one shows an actual number of letters in a particular sentence. The other shows an approximate percentage calculated from counting the numbers of letters in many sentences.

As you have already seen from answering the questions on page 24, the frequencies of the letters are similar in both bar charts. The two charts do not, match exactly, however.

● Which chart do you think is the most accurate?

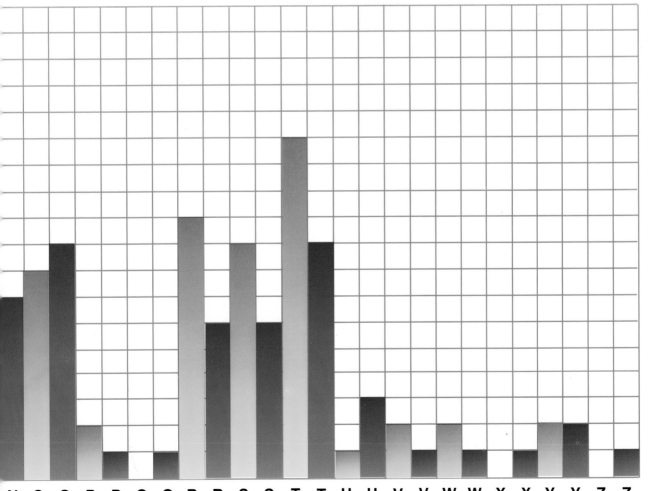

N O O P P Q Q R R S S T T U U V V W W X X Y Y Z Z

Cracking Substitution Ciphers

Each language has its own characteristics. If the letters of enough sentences are tallied to find their frequencies, the order of frequency of the letters for that particular language can be found.

The order of frequency for English is:

E T O A N I R S H D L C W U M F Y G P B V K X Q J Z

The most common three-lettered words are THE and AND.

For German the order is:

E N R I S T U D A H G L O C M B Z F W K V P J Q X Y

For French it is:

E N A S R I U T O L D C M P V F B G X H Q Y Z J K W

Once you know the order of frequency of the letters in the language in which a code is written, it helps you to decode any substitution cipher

This message is written in English.

**54 32 51 41 11 22 22 51 34 42 44
41 53 35 43 54 32 51 35 51 23 23**

You can crack the code.

● **1.** Look at the way the numbers are grouped. They are in pairs, which gives you a clue as to which type of code has been used.

● **2.** The pairs are also grouped. Two groups of three have the same numbers. What word might this be?

● **3.** What is the number pair that has been used the most times in the message? What does it probably represent?

● **4.** What does the message say?

If the message is sent like this, it is more difficult to decode.

**44 11 22 22 51 34 41 53 35 43 35
51 23 23**

E could be **22, 51, 35,** or **23,** and there are no word groups to give you a clue. But it is still pretty easy to crack the code.

●**5.** What is the new message?

Transposition Ciphers

42

You can make a good cipher by simply moving the positions of the letters in the message. This is called a transposition cipher

This is one way of doing it.

Rail Fence Cipher

Write out the message as if you are painting it on a rail fence.

Write out the top letters first, then the bottom letters to get:

RIFNEOEALECCD

What does this message written in rail fence cipher say?

MPNERTRWRNEKAISCEDAEIDS

☆ **Hints**

● **1.** How many letters are there in the message?

● **2.** Where do you think the bottom letters begin?

● **3.,** Draw a fence to write the message on so that you can read it.

Factor Grids

You can make a grid in which to put the letters of a message.

Suppose you want to say **THIS IS MORE COMPLICATED**

First count up the number of letters in the message. This message has 21 letters. Think of the **factors** of 21. They are 3 and 7. You can have a grid of three rows and seven columns or one of seven rows and three columns.

T	A	M	O	M	S	T
E	C	P	C	O	I	H
D	E	L	E	R	S	I

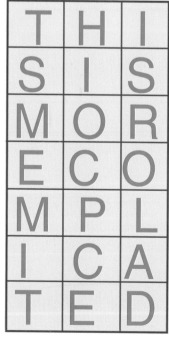

T	H	I
S	I	S
M	O	R
E	C	O
M	P	L
I	C	A
T	E	D

You can now write out the ciphered message several different ways.

If you use grid 2, here are four of the ways you can send the message.

You can write it another four ways, by starting at the end and going in the opposite direction.

Of course the receiver needs to know which route through the grid the sender has used.

● **1.** How many different grids can you send the message **JENNY SAFE** using this kind of grid cipher?

● **2.** How many different can you use for this message?

BURIED TREASURE THREE PACES N FROM SUN DIAL

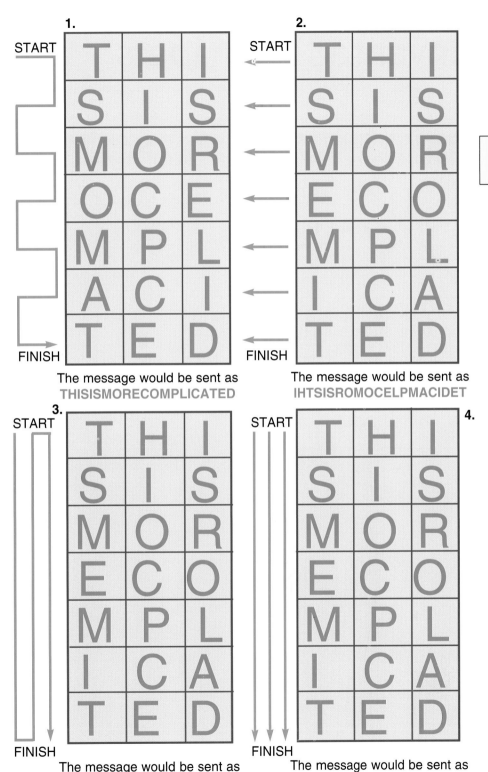

1.

START

FINISH

The message would be sent as
THISISMORECOMPLICATED

2.

START

FINISH

The message would be sent as
IHTSISROMOCELPMACIDET

3.

START

FINISH

The message would be sent as
TSMEMITECPCOIHISROLAD

4.

START

FINISH

The message would be sent as
TSMEMITHIOCPCEISROLAD

Invented Alphabets

46

One way to send coded messages is to invent a new alphabet.
This one was used in England until the 16th **century.**

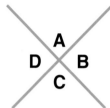 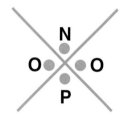

If a noble was hiding a priest in a priest hole in his manor
house he might send this message:

F   A   T   H   E   R   S   A   F   E

Try to make up your own alphabet. You will need 26 **symbols.** They should be easy to write, different from each other, and easy to remember.

This alphabet uses astrological signs and looks very mysterious.

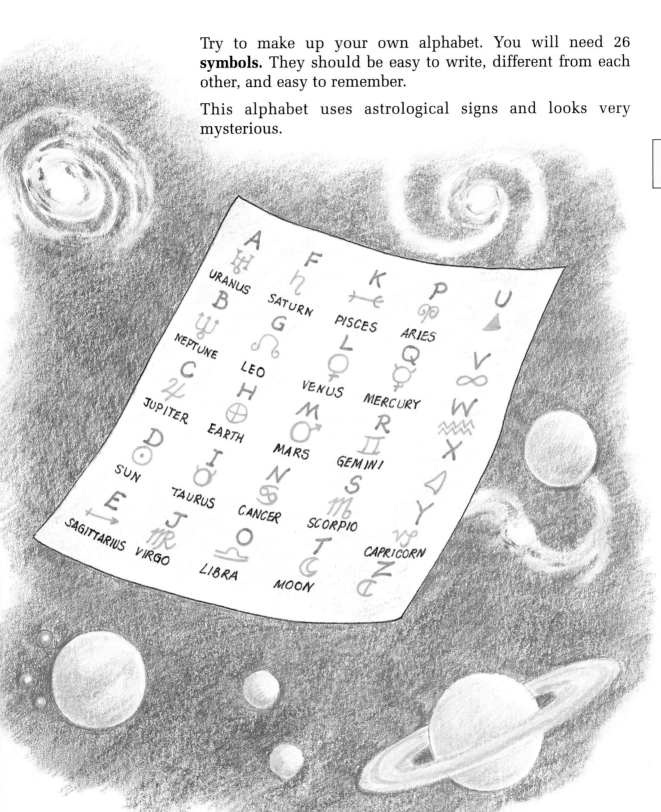

Braille

Not all invented alphabets, codes, and **ciphers** are used for secrecy. Here is a well known example of a kind of code:

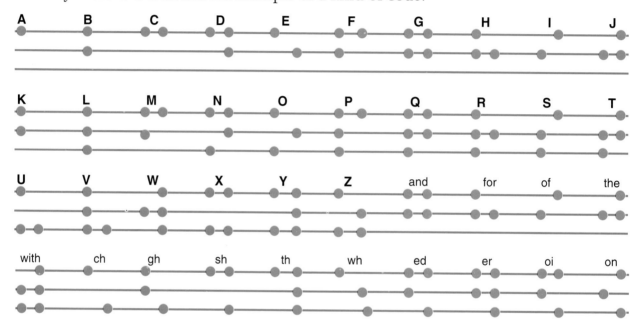

This is a system of raised dots for letters. It was invented by Louis Braille (pronounced *Brael*), and it enables blind people to read and write. Braille also has some other patterns of dots, which have not been shown, for specialist and technical **vocabulary.**

Braille used a 3 by 2 rectangular grid as the basis for his code. Each space either did or did not have a raised dot.

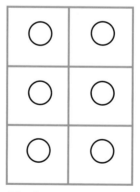

The basic Braille grid.

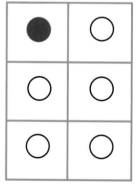

The code for **A** is one raised dot in the top left hand corner.

The number of dots and their positions determines their meaning. The code is read by running finger tips over the dots.

Braille was blinded when he was three years old after an accident playing with his father's tools. He invented the Braille system of raised dots at a special school for the blind when he was 15 years old, and he perfected the system in 1834 while he was teaching at a school for the blind in Paris.

One dot can be placed in six positions in a 3 by 2 grid.

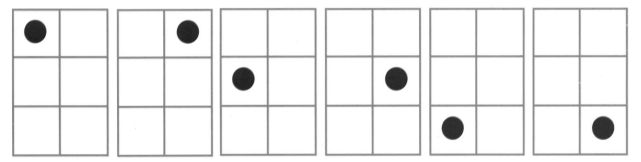

Braille used only one of the ways in his basic set of letters, sounds, and words.

● Which position was it and what does it mean?

Investigation

● How many possible ways are there of placing dots in a 3 by 2 grid?

☆ **Hints**

1. Try to have a system of working through the possibilities. One way is to find all the ways for one dot, two dots, and so on.

2. Record your results carefully. Check for repeats. Look for **reflections.**

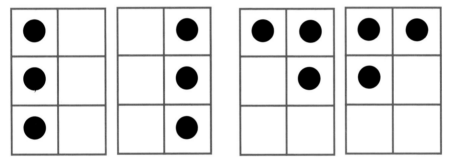

Examples of reflections

3. Make a table of results and look for number patterns. This is one way of doing it.

	NUMBER OF WAYS
0 DOTS	
1 DOT	
2 DOTS	
3 DOTS	
4 DOTS	
5 DOTS	
6 DOTS	

Morse Code

Samuel Morse invented a code in 1838 to send messages by telegraph. His code was especially good for this purpose because it needed only one wire. Earlier attempts to send messages through **telegraph** wires had used one wire for each letter of the alphabet.

Morse based his code on short and long buzzes. When the code is written out, a dot represents a short buzz and a dash a long buzz. When Morse code became widely used, S.O.S. was chosen as an international distress signal because the combination of three dots, three dashes, and three dots is easy to transmit and recognize in Morse code.

The alphabet in Morse code

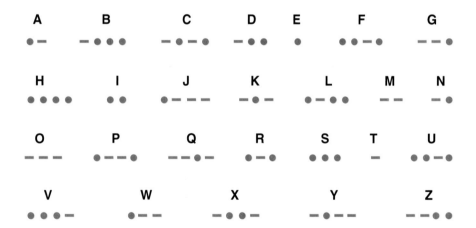

● **1.** In Morse code, how many letters can be represented by a single buzz?

● **2.** Why are E and T the letters represented by a single buzz?

● **3.** Two buzzes can be • • or – – What else can they be?

● **4.** How many different letters can two buzzes stand for?

52

Copy this table and fill in the blanks.

NUMBER OF BUZZES	NUMBER OF LETTERS	WAYS OF ARRANGING	
1	2	• —	
2	?	• — ?	? — —
3	8	• • • • • — • — • — • •	? ? ? ?
4	?	?	

● **5.** What number pattern do you see in the second column?

● **6.** How many letters can you make with five buzzes?

Bar Codes

One place where you might not expect to see codes is the grocery store. Many stores now use bar codes, which you can find on most items you buy.

The code is made up of black and white lines that can be scanned by a laser beam and translated into pulses of electric current for a computer to read. Each product has its own code. You can read it in numbers underneath the lines.

The computer keeps a record of each product it scans. This helps store owners to know how much they have sold and what stock they need to order. Some cash registers have scanners for reading prices from bar codes. Using a scanner is much faster than having to punch in each number on the old style cash register.

Now that you have investigated codes, you will start to notice them in all kinds of places. You can think of the **symbols** on weather maps and road maps as a kind of code. The Dewey decimal system uses numbers to sort books in the library by subject. A sheet of music is also a kind of code.

Have fun inventing, using, and finding codes!

Answers to page 45

1. You can send the message 16 ways.

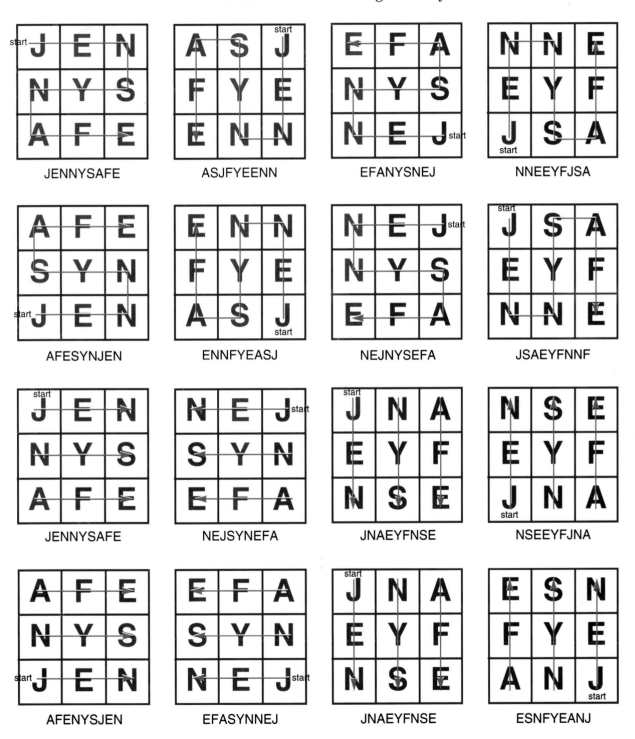

Answers to page 45

2. The message contains 36 letters, so look for the factors of 36. They are 2, 3, 4, 6, 9, 12, and 18. There are seven possible grids.

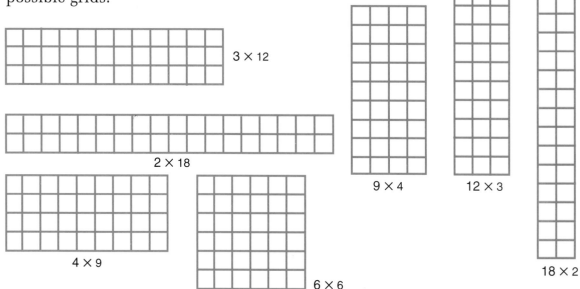

3 × 12

2 × 18

4 × 9

6 × 6

9 × 4

12 × 3

18 × 2

Answers to page 54

You can place dots 63 ways in a 3 by 2 grid.

This is one way of working it out:

There are six ways of placing one dot. (See page 49).

There are six ways of placing five dots. The ``no dot'' space can be in six positions. You can think of it as the opposite to the one dot pattern.

There is one way of placing six dots.

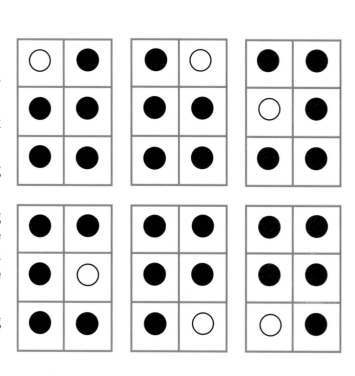

You can arrange two dots 15 ways. One way of making sure you do not miss or repeat any of the ways is to consider all the ways of putting another dot with a dot in a fixed position.

In line 1, the red dot in the top left hand corner is fixed. There are five places where the other dot can go.

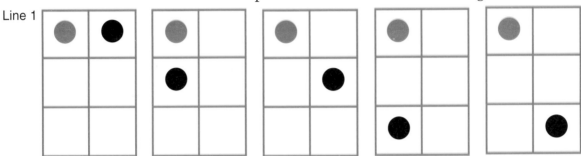

Line 1

In line 2, the red fixed dot moves to the top right hand position. There are now only four places where the other dot can go. It cannot go in the top left hand corner because that combination of dots has already been used in line 1.

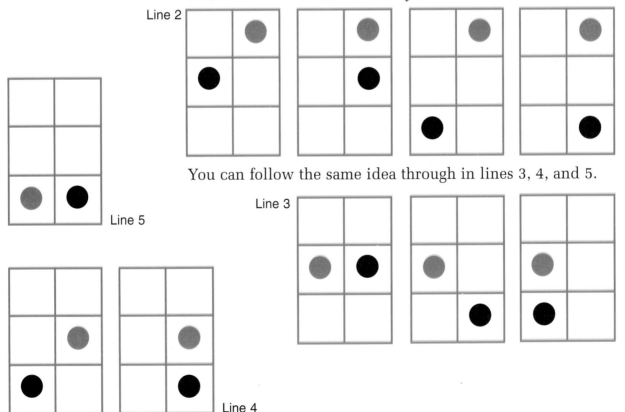

Line 2

You can follow the same idea through in lines 3, 4, and 5.

Line 5

Line 3

Line 4

You can think of arranging four dots as the opposite of arranging two dots. The spaces become dots and the dots become spaces.

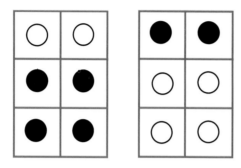

You can now fill in most of your table.

	NUMBER OF WAYS
	1
0 DOTS	6
1 DOT	15
2 DOTS	
3 DOTS	15
4 DOTS	6
5 DOTS	1
6 DOTS	

It is nearly complete. You can see that it is **symmetrical.** Unfortunately, that does not help to fill in the missing row.

If you have done other investigations of number patterns, you may recognize the sequence of numbers 1   6   15, 15, 6, 1. They are in Pascal's triangle.

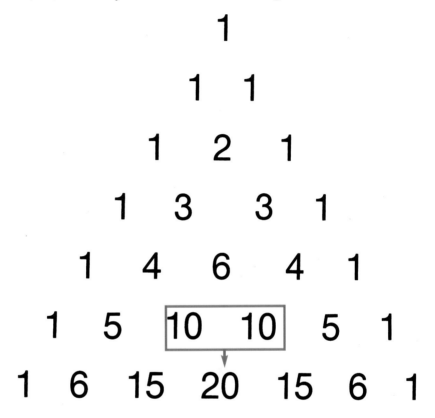

The triangle is formed by writing 1's at the ends of each line and adding the pair of numbers in the row above. You can see from the triangle that the missing number is 20.

The alternative is to draw all the ways of using three dots.

We don't count the one way of using no dots, add up the ways of using one, two, three, four, five, and six dots, to arrive at a total of 63 ways of using dots in a 3 by 2 grid.

Glossary

century a period of one hundred years. The 16th century goes from 1501 to 1600.

cipher a secret system of arranging the letters of a message

circumference the line around the edge of a circle

code a system that uses other letters or signs to stand for words

factor a number that divides another number into equal parts. 1, 3, 7, and 21 are factors of 21; 5 is not.

frequency the number of times an event occurs

null a dummy letter in a coded message that is not part of the message

radius the distance from the center to the circumference of a circle

reflection the mirror image of a shape or pattern

sector a part of a circle made by drawing two lines through the center of the circle, each line going from one point on the circumference to another point on the circumference

symbol a shape or sign used to stand for a letter or a word

symmetrical a pattern is symmetrical if one part is an exact reflection of the other

substitution cipher a way to disguise a message by replacing one letter with another in a regular way

telegraph a system of long distance communication using electrical signals along wires

vocabulary a group of words

Answers

Page 7
See page 8

Page 8
1. Lisa's message says, ``Meet me at Turnbull's yard at seven o'clock tonight.''
2. Leaving out the spaces between the words removes some of the clues that help someone else to work out what the message says.
3. This is how your message should look.

MEET FMEF ATFT

URNB ULLS

FYAR DFTO

NIGH TF

Page 9
The missing letters are J, K, W, and Y.

Page 11
1. QRVXU NSANF XRUND SSRXN XNSVZ QX
2. There are 24 letters and 3 nulls. You could have nine groups of three letters or three groups of nine letters.
3. Need reinforcements.
4. I shall fight at first light.
5. Have captured the Gauls' leader. (This has been grouped in sixes with O as a null to mark the end of a word.)

Page 17
1. A will become F.
2. Twenty-one spaces (26 − 5)
3. There are 25 possible codes. A can be any one of the other 25 letters of the alphabet.

Page 18
DIAM Ⓐ ONDS Ⓐ RECEIVED Ⓐ SAFELY

Page 19
1. Move each letter five places.
2. Where would you take a sick horse?
3. To a horsepital!

Page 20
1. See page 21
2. The code letter for **A** is **S**, and the code letter for **S** is **A**.
3. Yes, the same thing happens. **O** is the code letter for **E**, and **E** is the code letter for **O**.
4. The code letter for **W** is **W**.
5. Yes, the code letter for **J** is **J**.
6. There are twelve letters between **W** and **J**.

Page 21
1. There is an extra code on the counter-clockwise wheel because when A is the code letter for A, all the other letters are different.
2. None of the pairs of letters are the same on both wheels.
3. F and W are interchangeable.
4. Yes.

Page 22
1. B matches **B**, and **O** matches **O**.

61

2. None.

3. C matches **C**, and **P** matches **P**.

4. No.

5. Thirteen. Only moves of an even number of spaces give matching pairs. 26 ÷ 2=13.

62

Page 23

1. Twenty six

2. You can agree on a number to turn the wheel, or you can show the letter for A as a null in an agreed position in the message.

Page 26

1. What bet can't ever be won?

2. The alphabet

3. He had nobody to go with.

Page 27

The question is ``If it takes ten men four days to dig a hole, how long will it take five men to dig half a hole?''

The answer is ``There is no such thing as half a hole.''

Page 28

1. Z will be 26 × 3 = 78.

2. What's worse than finding a worm in an apple?

3. Finding half a worm

4. If you use division, you will have to use fractions or decimals for some of the letters.

Page 29

1. Multiply by 5 and subtract 3.

2. Subtract 1 and multiply by 4.

3. Add 3 and multiply by 2.

4. What do you get if you cross a snowball with a shark? (Use code 2)

Answer 20 68 56 72 76 4 32 76 16

Page 30

1. The numbers go up in fives.

2. The numbers go up in fours.

3. The numbers go up in twos.

Page 31

1. Question: If a dog is tied to a rope fifteen feet long, how can it reach a bone thirty feet away?

2. The numbers go up in fours.

3. 4 stands for A.

4. Answer: The rope isn't tied to anything.

Page 32

1. There are 26 letters in the alphabet and only 25 squares in the grid. One of the rarely used letters has to be omitted.

2. 51435133554442223545141

Page 33

1. The distance between the first of each group of letters is the same as the circumference of the tube required.

Page 35

The largest number is 18.

Page 37

1. The total of all the percentages should be 100.

Page 38

1. The four most frequent letters in English are, in order, E, T, A, and O.

2. The eleven least used letters are

B,F,G,J,K,P,Q,V,W,X, and Z.
3. The four most frequent letters in the sentence on page 14 are E, T, R, and O. R is not one of the four most frequent English letters.
4. The eight least frequent letters in the sentence on page 14 are B, J, K, Q, X, and Z, which do not appear at all, and F and U which are each used once. Then there are five letters which have a frequency of two.
The eleven least frequent letters in the chart on page 23 are B, F, G, J, K, P, Q, V, W, X, and Z. They each have a frequency of 1 percent.
The odd one out from page 14 is U, which has been used less frequently than it often is.

Page 39
The percentage chart is more likely to be accurate because more letters have been counted.

Page 41
1. A grid code has probably been used.
2. THE or AND
3. 51, E
4. The dagger is down the well.
5. Dagger down well

Page 43
Map in secret drawer in desk
1. 23
2. After K, the twelfth letter
3. M P N E R T R W R N E K
   A I S C E D A E I D S

Page 45
See pages 55 and 56.

Page 49
The raised dot is positioned at top left of the 3 by 2 grid. It means **A**.

Page 52
1. Two letters – a short or a long buzz.
2. Because they are the most frequent letters.
3. • – or – •
4. Four letters – two shorts, two longs, short and long, or long and short.

The completed table:

NUMBER OF BUZZES	NUMBER OF LETTERS	WAYS OF ARRANGING	
1	2	•	
		–	
2	4	• –	• •
		– •	– –
		• • •	• – •
3	8	• – •	– – •
		– • •	
		– • •	– – –
		• • •	• – •
		• – •	– – •
4	16	• • –	
		• • – –	– – • •
		• – • –	– • • •
		• – – •	– • • •

5. The number doubles each time.
6. Thirty-two letters (2 × 16 from the row above)

Page 54
See page 56.

Index